SURVIVING PRISON

SURVIVING PRISON

A Realistic/No-Nonsense Guide

by:

Hex,

The Helpful Ex-Con

Copyright © 2018 Hex, The Helpful Ex-Con

All rights reserved. No part of this book may be reproduced in any form or by any electronic or mechanical means, including information storage and retrieval systems, without permission in writing from the publisher, except for reviewers, who may quote brief passages in a review.

ISBN 9781726708418: Paperback edition

Cover art by: oliviaprodesign

For my wife. Through all the years, and all the ups and downs, you have always stood by me. You are the one who helped me learn what it is to be free. I love you baby.

Table of Contents:

Introduction

Chapter I: *So, You've Been Arrested*

Chapter II: *County Jail*

Chapter III: *What To Expect With Your Case*

Chapter IV: *Sentenced to: County Jail*

Chapter V: *Sentenced to: Prison*

Chapter VI: *Sentenced to Jail/Prison*

Chapter VII: *Doing the Time*

Chapter VIII: *Sexual Assault*

Chapter IX: *Suicide Awareness*

About the Author

Useful Websites

Hex, *The Helpful Ex-Con*

Introduction

My name is Hex, the helpful ex-con, and if you are reading this, then your life has taken an unexpected turn. Whatever the circumstances that brought you to my book, I hope things work out for you in the end. The reality is, you have some things that you have to go through before all of this is behind you. I think I can help, at least with some of it.

I am a 45-year-old, ex-prisoner, MWI (having married my prison pen-pal), valid Passport holder, father, and employed/taxpaying citizen. I have an "A" prefix, (meaning I was convicted and sent to prison one (1) time), and I have never been arrested again.

I have many felony convictions, ranging from receiving and concealing stolen property to selling drugs, and then on to shooting someone during an armed robbery. My felonies span from 1987 (when I was 14yrs old), until my last conviction(s) in 1994, that sent me to prison.

I was in and out of drug rehabs and the local juvenile detention facility as a teenager. As an adult, I was locked up from 18-20yrs old for selling drugs. And then I was 6 weeks away from my 21st birthday when I robbed and shot someone. I served over 13 years, 3 months in prison for that crime, and that is the one that changed me. I was paroled in 2007 and discharged 24 months later, without ever having a single violation.

During my incarceration, I was housed everywhere from a minimum security "Camp", all the way up to Level 4 (one level below "max" in my state). I was 21 years old, 148lbs, Caucasian, male, and very scared when I went in, though I hid it as best I could. I managed to survive my entire sentence without being raped, or having to kill someone. I was assaulted and cut, early in my sentence, and I learned how to avoid that from happening again, without becoming an informant.

I survived until I learned to succeed, within the walls and fences of prison. I did this by developing a philosophy that I will share with you. You may need to re-read some sections, as I tend to view things from a different perspective, and sometimes this may take some getting used to.

Family/friends/loved ones:

My parents were left helpless, watching me and my brothers run wild and go to jail/prison. So I am sympathetic to the loved ones of the incarcerated, I want to make that clear from the beginning. However, this book wasn't written with you as my primary audience. I wrote this book as if I was speaking to myself-and my friend group, back then, and I am saying what I wish I would have been told.

DISCLAIMER:

I am not a lawyer, nor do I pretend to be. Therefore, this book will not be advising anyone on legal strategy, or the merits of cooperating with the authorities. You, and your defense attorney are the only people that can help you with that.

My advice is what worked for me. Your own personal situation may differ, and you will have to make your own way. If you get nothing else from my words, take this with you.

Life is about "choices and consequences". If you do not like the consequences of your choices, then make different choices.

Hex, *The Helpful Ex-Con*

Chapter I:

So, you've been arrested.

Getting arrested is one of the most traumatic experiences a person can face. Once those cuffs click home, you have absolutely no-control over your fate.

But you DO have control over your own actions at this time. You have the right to remain silent, and you should exercise that right. You do not have to be rude. You do not have to be disrespectful. All you say is "I want to speak to an attorney", and not another word. Do not say anything, at anytime, to anyone, other than YOUR OWN PERSONAL DEFENSE ATTORNEY!

There is no standard for what exactly happens when you arrive at the police station. But, if you are under arrest, you can expect certain things. This list is not exhaustive, and jurisdictions differ. In no particular order:

- You will be searched. You will have to give up your jewelry, money, everything else you have in your possession.

- You will have your picture taken.

- You will have your fingerprints taken.

You will be placed in a cell. That may be a single person cell, with only you. Or that may mean a 30+ man drunk tank, or any other temporary detention.

- You will be given a phone call.

- You will be fed (depending on how long you are there before transferring to the County Jail).

- You may have a payphone in the cell that you can use, for collect calls, whenever you want. Or you may be taken out, one at a time, to use the phone. Doesn't matter, either way you need the same things:

    ○ Bail money

    ○ Lawyer

Hopefully, you are able to come up with both, and bond out. But if you are not able to post bail, shutting your mouth until your arraignment is your job. The arraignment is supposed to be 48 hours after arrest, 72 hours if arrested on the weekend. There are many reasons why this may not happen for you. While the law specifically states time-frames, it also allows for exceptions.

Whether your own personal courtroom delays are legal or not, does not matter. You need to view every moment from now on as potentially being used against you. Jails have camera's everywhere in the facility, both visible and not visible. You have to assume that you are being watched at all times.

Why does this matter? Because, maybe YOUR delay in YOUR arraignment is because someone is trying to provoke you. Police officers and Courtroom officials are people too, with all the same pettiness that the rest of us have. Maybe you were arrested on Friday and were supposed to be arraigned on Monday. But YOU weren't. Late afternoon comes around and the County van arrives, but YOU don't get on it. YOU wait for everyone else to ride out and eat your bullshit City Jail dinner in peace and quiet. At least until the nights arrests arrive. What do you do?

Well, before you do anything, and I mean ANYTHING, think first. No throwing your food tray. No slamming the phone, or otherwise damaging Government property. Both of these could result in a new charge, all before you got arraigned on this one.

See what they did there?

Stay calm. Stay quiet. Do not discuss your case and be careful with other people listening to your conversation. At some point, you WILL be arraigned and sent on to the County Jail, assuming you do not post bail or receive a PR bond. (Basically, they let you out after you promise to come back to court. If you don't show up, your financial life just got a lot more complicated.)

Chapter II:

County Jail

County Jail is typically used for short-term incarceration, usually 12 months or less. Any sentence of longer than a year is usually served in "prison", rather than County Jail. With prison closings, and overcrowded conditions, a person can find themselves serving a much longer portion of their sentence in the County Jail, depending on their jurisdiction. County Jails are loud, dirty, and aggravating in almost every way. The sounds, smells, and just the people in general, are things that you never forget.

Hopefully, you are not a drug addict, because if you are, it is going to be a rough few days. Medical services ARE available in County, and Emergency services are available 24hrs a day. But this is a County Jail and not a drug rehab. Non-life-threatening conditions will be dealt with as non-life-threatening conditions. So, unless you are a very bad drug addict, in a very serious condition, you will probably have to suffer through it.

Your pre-conviction County Jail time should be spent in silence, as regards your case. Do not talk in letters or phone calls. Letter's are read, and phone calls are recorded and if it is not "Attorney/Client Privilege", then those words and admissions WILL be used against you in court. Speak only to your Attorney. If you can not afford one, one will be appointed to you, by the courts. Speak ONLY to this person, I cannot stress that enough.

Remember, any fighting/contraband/violation of rules, WILL make you look worse in court. Don't stack more problems on top of yourself by acting out, this is what they want. Self sabotaged/prolonged incarceration reads as "Job Security" to the guards. Don't let them put their kids through College because you are easily provoked.

SURVIVING PRISON: A Realistic/No-Nonsense Guide

Chapter III:

What to expect with your case

There is no way for me to explain what is going to happen in your own, unique case. But there are some common things:

- Your arraignment: basically the State, publicly stating your charges.

- Preliminary Hearing is when they decide whether there's enough evidence to bind you over to Felony Court, or keep you in Misdemeanor Court. (Difference between Community Service and Probation, and Jail/Prison time.)

- Plea Hearing is where you enter a plea of guilty or not guilty. NOTE: If you are pleading guilty, based on a sentencing agreement that you have made with the

Prosecution, then you MUST say this ON THE RECORD. The judge will ask you something like "has anyone threatened you, or PROMISED you anything to cause you to plead guilty?" At that time, you say YES and explain the agreement you have made. If the judge does not want to agree to it, they will reject your plea. But if you DO NOT say it, ON THE RECORD, then the agreement NEVER HAPPENED. Please re-read that, because it is extremely important that you understand this. You can not appeal your case/sentence based on the judge going outside of a "Plea Agreement" that was never stated on the record. To put it simply, if YOU don't say it, the judge will NEVER know of it.

- Trial, and all the accompanying court appearances. There are many and going to trial is sometimes a very long and scary process. I personally went to trial on my assaults while facing life on two charges.

- Sentencing. This is where you find out your fate. If you were lucky enough to get out on bond, you may be "remanded to jail" immediately after hearing your sentence. Meaning, you go to jail right then and begin your sentence. For a very lucky few, they will be able to leave sentencing with a date to report to prison. This never happened to me, but it is rumored to happen sometimes.

- Sentencing usually ends up with one or more or the following:

- Fines

- Community Service

- Substance Abuse Treatment

- Mental Health Treatment

- Classes (parenting, anger management, etc.)

- Probation

- Jail time (day(s), weekends, week(s), month(s), up to 12 consecutive months total, usually.

- Prison time. One year–plus one day to Life/Death.

The main thing to remember through all of this is, we are not one incident. We made a bad choice, and are now facing the consequences for that choice, whatever they may be. The good thing about sentencing is you will know what you face. Whatever it may be, you will know.

Chapter IV:

Sentenced to:

County Jail

County Jail sucks, there is no way to sugarcoat it. And if you were looking for happy, happy, stories about inmates have 300 cable channels and all the crazy stuff you heard politicians say on the TV, well you were lied to.

County Jail is typically divided into two sections (for the general population prisoners, anyway).

- Those who are still waiting to be sentenced.
- Those who have been sentenced to serve County Jail time.

Those still waiting to be sentenced generally do not have many privileges.

- You may or may not have outside yard time.
- You may or may not have inside gym time.
- You may or may not have library time.
- You DO have phone time. You DO have visiting hours.

These things differ, depending on where you are locked up. But, generally speaking, those who are still awaiting sentence are doing boring time, in a loud and sometimes rowdy housing units.

Those who were sentenced to serve County Jail time, typically have a lot more privileges.

- Work–prisoners who are sentenced may be allowed to work as a "trustee", spending several hours a day working outside of their housing units. They may or may not be paid in money, but there is usually some type of compensation (extra food, extra time off their sentence, etc.) Or at the bare minimum, having a job allows you to be out of your cell and will help you walk each of those long days of your sentence.
- Yard time–you may or may not have yard.
- Gym time–you may or may not have gym.
- Library time–you may or may not have library time.
- Other services include:
  - Medical
  - Dental (may not be available in all jurisdictions).
  - Religious

- Mental Health (may not be available in all jurisdictions).

Generally speaking, County Jail is better than the City lockup, but it is still some of the worst time you can imagine. Just stressed out/mind numbing boredom. Best to stay away.

Chapter V:

Sentenced to:

Prison

Quarantine:

Your state may call it something different, but mine called it Quarantine. It is your first stop when leaving the County Jail and coming to prison. It is here that you will receive:

- prison identification number.

- medical screening (HIV/AIDS/STD testing, Mental Health, discussion of medical conditions and possible needed medications.)

- classification (risk assessment). They look at a number of things including:

    ○ severity of crime

- violent/non-violent
- age at time of offense
- prior record
- whether you were Honorably Discharged, or not, from the military.
- any other criteria the Department of Corrections that you are dealing with, chooses to use.

During classification, they look at all of their criteria and decide what security level prison is appropriate for you. A long time ago, where you lived was considered when placing you. They tried to keep you as close to home as they could, reasoning that the closer they are to home the more visits they will get. And with something to lose for bad behavior (visits) the prisoners are more prone to follow the rules. And then the prison population exploded, and they had to stop trying to accommodate, and just try to get everyone a bed.

Once they decide where they are going to send you, you wait for your transfer. They probably will not tell you when you are leaving, or where you are transferring to. They, generally speaking, do not release this information, for security purposes. But, every once in a while, you run into a guard who, if you aren't an asshole or a constant problem, may tell you. It has happened to me with a guard I have never met before, and also, once from a guard I knew. It doesn't hurt to ask, and the worst they can say is "no". Well, I guess that isn't true. The worst they could say is probably something a lot worse. But if you say something that causes a guard to verbally assault you, you might want to work on your "reading the temperature of the room", abilities.

Chapter VI:

Sentenced to:

Jail/Prison

Interacting with other prisoners.

The cold/hard reality of prison life is it is all about race. It is that way by design. How else could a few hundred corrections officers be able to control a prison population of thousands? Keep us divided and at each other's throats, and we are easy to manipulate.

However you were raised, whatever racial background you may have, none of that matters now. Leave, all of your politically correct ideas about a perfect society, at the curb on the night of your arrest. For your own safety.

Prison is a society, WITHIN a society. Small cities with economies both legal and underground (just like the "free" societies of the world), schools, jobs, stores (both legal and underground), drugs, booze, sex. People tend to believe that when someone is sent to prison, they just disappear or something. That whole "out of sight, out of mind" mentality. But, common public beliefs aside, that just is not the reality. We are still here, and we had to find a way to live around each other, without playing stab-em-up every day. Killers, car thieves, racists, sex offenders, and even all of you drunk drivers, all in the same cramped cells.

Here is a list of things to always be aware of. This list is not exhaustive, and it is not an absolute. How YOU interact with other prisoners will determine how they treat YOU.

- Be respectful. Yes, I am talking about saying "excuse me, thank you, I appreciate it/that, etc.", and all of those other things. I can't stress this enough, in prison, treat people how you want to be treated. It may not work with everyone, there are assholes out there, but it WILL get you a reputation as always being respectful, and that is important. Don't confuse being "respectful" with being soft or weak. It cost me nothing to say "Excuse me Fella's", when walking up to a table/group of prisoners for, whatever reason.

- Keep your word, always and at all times. Never borrow something from the prisoner store (run by a prisoner), unless you ALREADY have the money in your account. If you do NOT have the money yet but you promise to pay, you have set yourself up to be attacked. Know that and understand that BEFORE you do it. That whole "I didn't know" thing, doesn't work anymore. We call that "on ass", when you borrow/gamble without any money in your account. Example: "Look at so-and-so over there at the Poker table, playing 'on ass'. Hope he doesn't lose." And he better not, or else some Hollywood Blockbuster craziness could come to his cell. Prison IS survivable. But this type of nonsense is only going to end with you in protective custody, or the infirmary. Consider yourselves warned. Choices have consequences!

- Keep a close circle of people you hang out with, and watch each other's backs. The more people you associate with, especially at the beginning of your time, the more problems you face. Stay away from the gangs and observe everything and everyone around you. But don't stare! Staring could start a confrontation, and being the new guy, you could be surrounded by danger and not even know it.

- Mind your own business. Do not get involved in other people's drama. Unless it is someone in your close circle of associates. Do not talk shit about other people behind their backs, especially when you are new. This is a common setup to trap a new prisoner and try to squeeze them. For money, or sex, or ……anything really.

- Be cautious around new people and don't be too friendly. Always ask yourself "why is this person talking to me". Never just assume a person has good intentions. You will find out the truth, but only too late. Pay attention. Watch and observe. Who hangs out with who? Why is this person from this group, now over there with that group? Why is it so quiet in the Chow Hall? Look for what IS "normal" from the moment you walk in, so that you will know what ISN'T normal when you see it. You can feel the tension, don't worry, that will be obvious. What you need to do is learn to be able to spot the move/play BEFORE it happens, so that you can make sure to be elsewhere when it goes down.

- Practice your "look". Yes, I mean that! Stand in your

mirror and practice going from all other facial expressions, straight to cold faced – dead-eye, stare. Sounds stupid and it will feel dumb when you do it, trust me. But after a few weeks, when you have it, you don't have to practice anymore. Get comfortable with this face and wear it a lot. You don't need to be so happy all the time, outwardly at least.

More times than I can count, my "prison face" saved me from experiencing violence. As I said in my intro, I am not a big guy, never have been. The biggest I got in prison, after years in the weight pit AND quitting smoking, was 178lbs. What can I say, I have a fast metabolism and I struggled for every ounce of muscle I obtained. But that is not how I survived. When situations come up and I put on my "prison face" with my calm and unafraid voice saying my practiced responses, it gives people pause. Especially if I was alone, and they were not. Don't get overly cocky or boisterous. Do be blunt and pointed, but not personally disrespectful. It is a balance, you will learn it. You don't have to be the hothead, but you can be. That way brings more possible fighting thought. Again, know that going into it. Choices have consequences.

Chapter VII:

Doing the time

There is an old prison saying "Do the time, don't let the time do you", or various versions of it. The meaning is simple, don't crumble under the weight of all of those years. The reality is a little more complicated than that though.

You have already been sentenced and are now either on the sentenced side of the County, or you are in prison. Either way, your sentence has begun, and the time doesn't stop. The problem is, prison clocks run at 1/3rd the speed of a normal clock. True fact! So, as a prisoner, you need to kill the hours.

- I recommend everyone to get a job (or start school, if you do not have your G.E.D). Any job that you will actually do. Get that job as soon as you can, so you can get more time out of your cell. Once you already have a job, you can try to transfer to another assignment later on. I like library jobs, always have. They are the "sleeper" jobs that most people don't think of. It has a lot of perks and is a quiet/low stress job, and you have first pick of all the books.

- Visit the library on a regular basis. It doesn't matter if it is the Law library or the regular one. (Unless you are appealing your conviction, then you need to be living in the Law Library every moment you can.) Go to the library and READ!

- Exercise regularly. You don't have to become a muscled up freak, but you SHOULD exercise. Prison is unpredictable and violence happens without warning. You could be attacked because someone owes money to someone they are afraid of, but they aren't afraid of YOU, so they attack you. Or a group of prisoners attacked someone, but you got caught up in it and now have to defend yourself. And if you haven't been taking care of yourself, you are going to lose that struggle. Exercise.

- Start all of your program recommendations as soon as possible! Send out kites (or whatever you call your prison messaging system), signing up for any AA/NA, therapy, schooling, and whatever other groups/classes you are required to take.

- Send in a Dental Appointment request as soon as you arrive at a new facility. Every time you ride in to a new facility. The dental call-out list is long, and I mean very long. It takes months to years to get in unless you have an emergency. So send in that request as soon as you arrive. And as soon as you receive dental care, put in another request. I averaged about one checkup visit, every 3-4 years, and I put in my requests just like I am advising all of you to do.

Well, that is enough of that for now, lets get to the nitty gritty. The everyday life that you have to adjust to.

- **Transfer bus.** I believe I should quickly discuss transferring, whether that is when you initially arrive at Quarantine, or transferring from facility to facility. Follow all commands by Transport Officer's. They have guns. They can shoot you. If they do, and they over-reacted, nobody will ever know. And you will still be dead. These officer's are usually a little rougher than the rest. The nature of the job I guess, always worrying about escape. Don't play games. Don't argue and/or act out in any way. Choices have consequences, and transport consequences are possibly fatal.

- **Cell-mate(s).** Unless you are assigned a single-man cell, all to your lonesome, you will have a cell-mate. Or "Bunky", as I always referred to mine. You will spend a great amount of time, locked up alone together, with your cell-mate(s). Racial issues, religious differences, age gap, education gap ….all of these things exist and must be addressed. No-matter the outside issues, you have to live together. And sleep in the same room together. And that takes a certain amount of understanding and trust.

Even if you and your cell-mate(s) do not like each other, having a violent conflict with your bunky is unwise and dangerous. The sleeping thing I mentioned, remember? If you have a cell-mate/bunky that you do not get along with, go to your prison Counselor (or whatever staff member is in charge of your housing unit), and request a cell change. The circumstances that you find yourself in, if you have to have this conversation, are impossible for me to predict. So my advice is, if you can, try to move without mentioning your bunky.

If all else fails, you can try to be grown-ups about it. I had a bunky who was beefing with my close associate. We both went to the Counselor and explained that we have too many personality differences to live together and one of us needed to move. This has worked another time for me when me and a guy just lived together for too long. We lived together, ate together, worked-out together, and were in the same class in school. Too much, and one of us had to go.

- **Yard/recreation buildings.** During yard/rec time, you have a lot of prisoners moving at the same time. There are not many guards around, though they are supposed to be paying attention when units go back and forth to yard. But with possibly hundreds of prisoners, it is best to not put your personal safety in another person's hands. Your safety is on you, so pay attention!

A good and healthy attitude to have is the belief that everything is your fault, in some way or another. There is not a single incident that could happen to you in prison where you cannot see where YOU put yourself in that position through your own choices. And choices have consequences. Just because you had every right to walk up to that picnic table and sit down, doesn't mean it was the smart thing to do. But since you don't pay attention and you think prison is a cartoon and nothing bad will ever happen to you, you sit down and get smashed. And then come with the "it's not my fault" garbage.

If you live with the "it's not my fault" attitude, nobody will respect you and they will treat you like a child. Or a bitch. Nobody wants to listen to a grown ass man whine and cry all the time. This behavior will cause you serious problems.

Pay attention to the picnic tables. It sounds petty, but certain groups/gangs may "claim" a table as their own, and if you use it you could have problems.

- **Weight rooms.** Pay attention when using the weight rooms. Alot of fights and assaults happen there, and with all the other prisoner's standing around, it is very difficult for the guards to see. You, and your work-out partners need to keep an eye out for unexpected surprises.

  Be respectful, and share equipment. If you want to be able to go borrow some dumbbells or other weight equipment, but never let anyone use YOUR equipment, you have already created the situation where you will get into a fight. You have already done that. Share the weights. If they ask and you aren't done, tell them to give you a minute, and wave them down when you are done. THIS advice will take you far, and I am not just saying that. Doesn't matter your race, age, or affiliation. If you are a straight up person in all things, they may not "like" you, but they will respect you.

  Be respectful of the equipment. The Prisoner Benefit Fund (or whatever your State calls it), paid for all the recreational equipment. That money comes from the prisoners themselves, through an added tax on store goods and other items order from an approved vendor's, fundraisers, etc. That money comes from YOU, so if you are a guy who breaks shit when he gets upset about something, stay the fuck out of the weight/recreation rooms. Choices have consequences.

- The #1 you need to know about prison is that it is for adults. There are rules that are enforced very swiftly and violence is always the punishment. It doesn't matter what your actual age is, behave as a grown-up at all times. Leave the games, wrestling matches, stealing, and playing to the kids and you have eliminated the most common causes of drama and misconduct reports that could affect your release date.

- **Library/Law Library.** The Law Library is a "right", and the General Library is a "privilege". It is important to know the difference.

   Federal law guarantees the right to access to the courts, meaning, you have the right to use the Law Library. Even though it is a right, breaking the rules will put restrictions on your access to it. With filing deadlines and all the requirements of filing a timely Appeal, you don't have time to waste on any type of restrictions, act accordingly.

- **General Library.** General Library is a privilege, 100%. anything that is a privilege, can be taken away. The most common causes of loss of privileges is misconduct reports (tickets, write-ups, whatever).

   One of the main things that helped me learn to stay out of trouble and stop clashing with the guards, is the library. A book has no commercials. A book can take you to a faraway place and show you sights you never dreamed. A book can teach you something you didn't know. And at a bare minimum, reading books will increase your vocabulary and reading ability. I went to prison with an 11th grade reading level, (according to my G.E.D test scores. After just 6 years of reading whatever interested me, my reading level jumped to 12+, (according to another test I took to become a tutor in the school).

   Some prisons have an actual budget that they spend on books, etc. Some prisons have no budget and rely on donations from charities to fill their shelves. And some prisons have no library at all. If you are lucky enough to be at a place with a well-funded library, get your read on!

I recommend everyone to go to the library, even if it is just to sit and read a magazine. Get a little quiet time and stay out of the mix for a little while. You will never look back at this time and regret not going to yard to watch some nonsense. But you MIGHT regret not going to the library.

- **Chow Hall/Cafeteria.** I will tell you what an "old head" told me when I first came to Quarantine: Always go last to meals (chow).

  It sounds backwards, right? Why would you want to go last, what if they run out of something? You are right, they could run out of something. But is it worth your life? In my time in prison, and even in the jail, chow line's are some of the most dangerous places to be.

- If you go last to chow:

  o You might not get that piece of cake you saw on the menu.

  o You might not be able to be first in line to whatever it is you have planned for after chow.

  o You might be hungry for a little while longer.

  o The chow hall is clearing out of people while you are eating, significantly reducing noise and making for a more relaxing experience.

- If you go first to chow:

  o You will probably get that piece of cake.

- You might even get something as a leftover from a previous meal.

- Tables are all empty when you get there, but fill up very fast all around you, surrounding you with people.

- Whatever beef is going on with other prisoners, will probably be settled in the Chow Hall, or to and from it. So, you have a pack of unknown violence who are coming up behind your unsuspecting self, and you may get caught in the middle of a situation that had nothing to do with you. For a piece of cake. Choices have consequences.

Chapter VIII:
Sexual assault

As men, we are not used to having to talk about sexual assault. But the reality is, men are the overwhelming majority of people who are doing the crimes. So it comes as no surprise that the hidden "truth" about rape, is that more men are raped in prison every year than women on the streets. That is a fact.

I am not going to tell you that rape does not happen in prison because that is obviously a lie. But, from what I have seen and heard, it isn't like what you think. They don't necessarily come attack you and try to rape you. At least that never happened to me, or people I knew. What DID happen, and what I saw happen in every prison, is they try to squeeze you. It isn't rape if you say yes. They scare you, try to trick you, send friends at you. They are relentless and seem truly unstoppable. But this isn't true.

There are many options available to you if you feel you are at risk of sexual assault, or have been assaulted. Going to staff is an option, and may even be the safest one for you. If that is the case, then go directly to the desk and tell them you have an emergency and need to see the nurse. Tell them stomach/heart/whatever, and fake it. This gets you out of the housing unit and away from the other prisoners. Tell the nurse and ask for protection. But don't come back. And if you are ever in another prison and see people who knew, avoid them like the plague.

Going to staff may not be an option for you. I understand. Be sure to observe exactly where all the camera's, and other surveillance equipment are located, so you know where to run to for safety. They don't want to be caught on tape doing that stuff, so remember where your safety areas are.

Each prison is different and there is no standard way to go. Things that will help you stay safe:

- Don't go to the shower alone if you can avoid it.

- Shower with your back to the wall. Never wash your face/hair in the shower. Do it in your sink. (In higher levels or dangerous situations.)

- Keep a new bar or two of soap, wrapped up in the clean t-shirt you brought with you. Keep it near you, do not let other people know or see. (In higher levels or dangerous situations.)

- Observe and figure out who the "predators" are and do not associate with them. For any reason. Once you give them an opening, they will not stop.

- Stay true and loyal to your close circle of friends. You all have each other's back, and there is safety in numbers.

- Do not put yourself in a situation(s) where your safety is compromised. Observe your surroundings and learn your environment. And if you feel something isn't right, it ISN'T! Trust your gut, it may just save your life.

Chapter IX:

Suicide Awareness

I did not feel that I could end this book without speaking about prison suicide.

Every person who has ever been to prison, has thought about committing suicide. I did, and so did every person I have spoken to about it. It is the one thing that we all have in common and truly binds us together – every day we woke up and chose not to kill ourselves.

I developed a philosophy very early in my sentence. It simply says that each morning I have a choice. I can:

- attempt escape
- commit suicide
- face today

Every morning I wake up and make a choice. Every morning, I

keep making a choice, hoping that one day I can put prison behind me. As long as I do not choose to kill myself, I have a chance to make another choice. Day after day, year after year, until one day, they let me go. I am not a doctor or a therapist. I am just a guy who went to prison at 21 and did 13+ years. During that time:

- I never attempted escape, not even once.

- I never killed myself, not even once.

- I never faced a day that was so bad that I would not face another, not even once.

I faced some of the worst times of my life while inside. The early year's, in high-level prisons, were tough. Violence against me. Violence all around me. Dirty, nasty, depressing, cockroach infested.....nightmare center's! And I never killed myself, not even once. There is a common public belief that prisons are just 24/7 torture chambers, but my own experiences have shown me that is not true.

You are being sent to prison AS punishment, not FOR punishment. Do you see the distinction? 5 years, 50 years, Life, or Death......THAT is your punishment. To be deprived of your rights, your freedom being the most visible, but only one of the rights you lose. Movies and television are not reality, at least not every single second of every single day.

I said that to say that I also had some of the BEST times of my life in prison. Even in the worst facilities imaginable, there is periodic humor. Sometimes even friendship and comradery although based on very tense situations.

Every day, no-matter how bad it was when I laid down on my bunk for bed, and it was pretty bad sometimes, I always chose to wake. And I always chose to face the new day. You can change your mind back and forth, face the consequences and try again if you choose, but only if you choose to live.

Life is about choices and consequences, that is what my incarceration taught me. Choices and consequences. Every thing that has ever happened to me, after I became an adult, is my own fault. The good and the bad, my choices brought it all. I had to learn how to assess risk and reward and decide if I am willing to face the consequences of this choice. If the answer is no, then I make a different choice.

People say that I have "changed" and that is not true. I didn't change, find God, re-invent myself or anything like that. I learned to make better choices, by looking past "right now" and seeing what my choices are going to bring. To me. To those around me, which will bring it to ME after it goes to THEM. Understand?

No-matter how bad you feel right now, you may feel differently tomorrow, but one choice could take away any tomorrow you may have had. If you are supposed to die, then make them kill you. It isn't your responsibility to rid the world of......you.

But if you REALLY feel bad for what you have done, and feel you have to do something, do what I did. I swore to myself to never create another victim. That the number of people that can claim to have been victimized by me, in any way, DOES NOT GROW!

And for the man I shot. No apology could ever replace from him what I took. I have never tried to contact him. To do so would be even more selfish than the crime itself, in my opinion, and I will not traumatize him, or his family again. Not in any way. So, despite the minimal effort required to buy another firearm, I will not. Because I will never put myself in a situation where I may end up having to choose whether to fire a gun at someone. Never. I will never pursue having my gun rights restored. I will never go shoot guns with buddies. And I will never have a firearm in my home. Nobody will ever experience what it is like to be harmed by me again.

And that is why I did not need to die. Because I meant it. And now, I am telling it to you. I don't know what you did, but there is a chance that my record is longer and my crimes are worse. And I did not need to die, and I believe I have, in some small way, started to deserve to live.

About the Author

I have been in trouble, in one form or another, since I was around 8 years old. I was a thief, a liar, and completely unreliable. I used drugs and drank from a young age, graduating to different crimes. Selling drugs. Selling fake drugs. Armed robbery. Shooting someone.

I met my wife on a pen-pal website, (actually, she found my ad), and we were together for the last 4 years of my sentence. We married shortly before I discharged from parole and have been together ever since. We did not live together after I got out and maintained a long distance relationship (with visits) until after I got off parole.

I have a valid passport, legally obtained, and I use it! I see places and experience things in my life today that I never dreamed possible when I was in prison. And all I did was learned to make better choices.

I chose to wait until now to write my "theories", although I have been itching to do so, for a long time. Viewing the free world through a "prison lens", as I do, I realized that I could not do this sooner. Much like an old prison number gives your words "weight", my time out here applies in the same way, in my opinion. I have been out of prison for over 11 years now, with no parole violations or new arrest. And despite my best efforts in self sabotage, I have not blown this chance. And I have never found myself climbing through a window, or pointing a gun at someone, so I believe I have this figured out. At least some of it, anyway.

My goal is to educate and guide prisoners (new and old) into adapting a new way of viewing the world. To show you how to flip things around and use your experiences to succeed in society. Because, in my opinion, criminals are uniquely qualified to surpass non-criminals in almost every way. The "normal's" believe that there is nothing good that can come out of crime. Let's let them keep thinking that, at least until all of you get out.

This is the first book in a series that will cover:

Surviving prison: Overview and advice on entering, adapting, and surviving prison.

Succeeding in prison: Making the most of your time. Schooling and fulfilling recommendations. "Institutional economies" and surviving on your own.

Relationships: Maintaining, strengthening, and repairing existing relationships. Pen-pals and building new relationships.

Pre-Release and Parole: What to know 2yrs/1yr before your release. Preparing for seeing the Parole Board. Release and surviving parole. Finding a job.

Life after parole: What comes next? Passports/travel. Legal hustles. Life.

Useful websites

Penpal websites:

https://writeaprisoner.com/

htttps://www.prison-penpals.net/

http://www.friendsbeyondthewall.com/

http://www.inmate.com/

https://www.meet-an-inmate.com/

The only one of these that I am familiar with is writeaprisoner. That is where I met my wife.

Support/Advice forums:

http://www.prisontalk.com/

After a google search, and some browsing, PTO is the only one I could find that has an "active" membership. Now, I didn't spend all night looking, but I looked at a bunch, and judging by the number of threads/post, PTO is my recommendation.

Hex, *The Helpful Ex-Con*

Made in the USA
Columbia, SC
04 November 2023